FLOWERS, ALL SOR..

FIGS, BERRIES, AND FRUITS

FORGOTTEN

OISÍN BREEN

Poems © Oisin Breen 2020

ISBN 978 1 873412 04 6

TABLE OF CONTENTS

ISN'T THE ACT

OF PLACING FLOWERS ON A TOMB

A GESTURE OF BRINGING

A LITTLE LIFE

BACK TO THE DEAD?

One

Memories, stilled and muted harmonia,
 silk-heavy in the russet wind,
 like sinuous leaves with ice-cracked spines,
 and a timbre of slowness,
In a schema of licentiousness,
Prompt, more so than age,
 these liver spots on my translucent skin.

      But the act itself,
      its flash powder of yellow-tan dust,
      engorges the hour-hand at it's brightest,
      in a languor reconstituted: all just variations of dusk --

And the end is composed of orchids,
 and the lopped heads of milkweed,
 sundered by centrifugal force:
 an effulgence of shadows,
 shimmering on sun-whetted stone.

And I place flowers on my father's grave,
 a gesture, like any other,
 to bring life to the dead.
And beside me two junkies eat a watermelon from a plastic bag,
And a black and white tit hops beneath their feet.

Now my palms are blanched in a pattern of earthveined rust,
 and as pebbles, indicative of meaning, litter the sky of sand,
 its absence is a comfort.

REMINISCE THEN IS THE CHARRING OF THE MOORLAND BY
INCESSANT HEAT.
IT IS THE LIMP NECK OF THE PIOUS GROUSE,
THE TRILLING NASAL SCRAWL OF ITS GRIEFBLIND MATE,
IT IS THE SNAPPED TETHER,
A SCHOONER GUIDED BY LEYLINES AND CAST ENTRAILS,
A TRANSUBSTANTIATED EUCHARIST OF THE INCHOATE

Accession here means there is nothing left but the one,
Rejection that not even the one remains.

Whist, I say.
Whist, I know.
Whist, I know and love you.

Two

This is a quilt-work composed of acts of forgetting,
 and each instance of kenning is a quickened sapling.

The variable alone brooks difference,
   as memories harden in the dermal layer.

This is what it means to be bereft,
 and with no ready mercy.

This is an altar for Harry Wasylyk,
  the patron saint of archways,
  whose polyethylene skin eschews grace for ennui,
  as he watches us slouch-hang our mouths into victuals of lilting
  lines of brutal song.

In 1925, the world changed.
A ritual, which became a practice, turned convenience,
And obscene, obtuse cylinders of black tar aped king rats,
Stook like monoliths where the mills rust.

Yet I placate my father's grave with calcite flowers,
Yet my grief is insufficient for I see it dissipate.
I am but missteps and false starts,
  a captured stillness that records my ill intent.

Yet I lack the wherewithal to fail to yield to the palpable thrum.
  It is extrinsic,
  and dressed in surges of undifferentiated starlight,
  I am asymptotic, and bifurcated in mnemonic flight,
  and each point is plotted in baroque notation,
  as plush woven sounds wash in the rippling coarse-grain of
  transition --

        Where phased space enacts a hallowing,
                in between the lines
        of porous stalks and motion begetting blooms.

Where slips in time--

     transitions--

Bring about only the hoary apocrypha of the Liffey Run,

Or the morning spent sleeping in Howth hedgerows,

     comforted by another man's shoes as our pillow.

My clothes hang heavy with the flavour of wet fire,

 and my limbs are contortions of intent as we stagger to the DART,

 and as the doors drearily clatter, rust-heavy in peeling greens,

 the pallor of wilful abuse, and intent, sputters to life,

but we wrap them archly in a sun-starved grin.

And the muck, it spirals out of us in duodecimal digits,

And I can thread you a death-mask in sea-spittle,

And your life is written in sea-spray on the hard lines of your

cheeks.

     TIRED OF THE WEIGHT

UNDER THE AEGIS OF LENGTH-FORGETTING TIME

     CIRCUMCISED, CULLED

     I GROW WEARY OF CONSTRAINT

     AND APPROXIMATE

And in turn each approximation,

Becomes the outline of the boundaries of the next,

And our plump history is sketched in non-linear distance,

 between the staple and the snare.

So our reveries prove little more than a drunkard's crutch,
a balalaika melody for a bleached autumnal prayer,
the fat-bellied surety of knowing
the origin is preceded by the end.

Three

It is only in death that the final form of those we loved emerges.
Though as we ourselves approach death, their shape intermingles with our
own changing.

I have a grá for you,
And a deep thirst,
And eyelids heavy with hunger.

And we see them again, the dead,
reinvented, despite an elegy of presence,
And I wonder will I see myself the same way when I go?

Once, aged 17, I drank from a bladder-pelt of cider, while turning in
circles with my friend's mother, and she was lovestruck with the sickly
sweetness of her son's menagerie, though she, and fitfully all of us, knew
that we'd more likely have the gutterslung luck of the dead in us than for
this to be more than just a procession of   moments in a broken nest of
long lives of airbrushed memories, even if rare bonds there continued to
coalesce.

Whist, I say. Whist, I know. Whist, I know and love you.

But what if I forget myself? or spend the days -- in truth -- with the mouth full of ash, observing a vertical/horizontal lattice of incremental anamorphoses between what might have been, to what was?

What if in transition I can but stoop through an archival perspective where the focal eye had but the rush of blood of common prey and the fortune-hungry haruspex prove not all-seeing, but all fearing, as the hareish thing then stamped her feet to warn us of the danger in the orchard as she a culling spun?

Perhaps then it is only possible to commit the cathecism in generations, when there is little left to say but that it was:

    catabiotic
        contingent,
            that ferment,
                an embodiment.

    But the act itself
    its flash powder of yellow-tan dust,
    engorges the hour-hand at it's brightest,
    in a languor reconstituted: all just variations of dusk-

This is but a history of contempt.

Four

I ask then of you these questions:

What maker stretched out melancholy,
  like a fattened pig's skin,
  into a parchment of minor regrets?

What constellation blasted drear light,
  a nova of turned down gas dials,
  into a litany of hot wind and frozen pipes?

What songbird hovered flightlessly,
  its wings silent, and its mouth open,
  precocious in a rendition of the vacuum?

What night, illuminated by the mossy green of old lamplight,
  its possibilities fragmenting like forming ice,
  sheds skin in recompense for a fallow wantonness on the lips?

What measure is this that strips us of compassion,
  but leaves us thrilling at the raspy fulsome pleasure of it all,
  a hot wet fungus in a crystalline dew?

I tell you, this is the glorifying numbness.

And, if I say that once, in the name of the Buckskin Doe,
  I sundered my free will,
What will you make of me?

I ask you, what day, lit by the heavy shadows of young starlight,
  its possibilities bonding like erupting earth,
  fuses atoms in lieu of the fertile chastity of silent tongues?

I ask you-
What do you make of me?

A golem,

A capitulation that spans and separates memory; a continuum of dry
leaves and dead air; piano notes –
Just silence in the rapture of the mulch.

Five

Three-times,
It was three-times it happened, and on the third day, I slew a cockerel just
to smooth its dried ochre in a paste over my thought-split eyes, to stem the
euphoric aurorae cleaving my perception of time, as I had a vision of the
potentate of the death of heat who's crystalline halitosis pushed a hot slag
through my star-burst skull and left me reeling-

Oh barû!

I can not ascertain your memories, nor your devotion, in the flight of your
birds.

It was three-times it happened, and on the third day, I tenderly caressed the whorls that trapped flakes of your skin, and the rough wood was a splendour for its history, a litany to passion, and a flood of colour left behind, but it was the better part of fear that led me to the boneyard where I revel in kisses shadow-caught.

I am the last living thing that remembers you.

Oh barû,

I can not know if you straddle moments, or if snake-like you strangle me in echoes of anamnesis. Nor do I trust you to forget, or to pigment the images you see, as I do, with figments of rent seas, even now, as you plunge your teeth into the entrails of your kin.

Oh barû,

I asked you for memory of my father's death, but you chose to lavish your bann, and I do not atone.

But Asipû,

In vigil, I ask you to forgive me -- you said it once to Sennacherib -- and so I too atone.

He that stilleth all to rest, that pacifieth all, by whose incantations everything is at peace, the gods are upon his right hand and his left, they are behind him and before.

Christ with me,
Christ before me,
Christ behind me,
Christ in me.

Six

We were barefoot because we had been in the sea,
and the nearby road was made of gravel,
and it hurt to walk on,
and the sorrows of the sea-cliffs punctured the dead air.

The roadside grass was taller than I was,
and I knew what I was doing was wrong,
but I was frozen in a giddy kind of fear,
        willing myself on.

I hid because there was a kid nearby I knew.
We all called him retarded.
I was bullied too, but hating him was a guilty treat.
I was happy to feel like everyone else.

I threw myself against the nearly white grass.
It was the strongest summer I had known.
I was in a Wexford caravan park.
I was hiding.

He was lost.

Not helping him meant peace.

The grass was hot; it pushed through my shirt, scratching my skin.

The sun had that technicolour quality, where it's all horizontal lines:

A vision of etoliated whiteness.

We were barefoot because we had been in the sea,

and the nearby road was made of gravel,

and it hurt to walk on,

and the sorrows of the sea-cliffs punctured the stillness.

I hid because in the final analysis, I was young.

I had placed a last act of submission above one of love.

Now, in memory, each breath scorches those left-behind footprints into a sculpture of invigorating presence and an eerie allotment of dumb abstinence.

Now, it is breached only by the skulking din of chattering teeth; a charter of trapped flies; and a grey decaying weave.

Now reverie is spun inverse as the needle snaps,

and I traverse the space of its hands,

and this is what constitutes the giving of names.

And by Cnoc Uisnigh -- her red hair for Conochobar of the reeds -- *when
she is old enough we'll* -- with raven's colours -- Naoise, Ardan and
Ainnle pinioned by a spear, they live like flowering weeds in the memory
of Deirde's head, it bashed to pieces against the soft calumny of rock.

Oh barû!

> The act itself,
> its flash powder of yellow-tan dust,
> it engorges the hour-hand at it's brightest,
> in a languor reconstituted: all just variations of dusk.

So I hid because I didn't know what else I could do.
  to continue as it is means to be forever harried by the past.
But the willing youth of me just tore at the lattice by candlelight.

Now I remember all this as just a hulking portent of a future where I
would have to act against myself just for the greater good, but full of a
fearfulness that the acting might become me.

And in a way it did.

I hid because fate is a way out,
and salty epiphanies are beautiful,
like rotten flowers in a fat glass,
  and wet Edinburgh streets.

And yet, there exist brief moments of rest,

Even now. Parabola,

As we dangle our feet upwards,

Towards the windbeswept cliffs and rocky shores.

And yet, there is a trace of shape in these refracted signals,

where laceworks of my own selfhood are pulled taut.

This is the pursuit of tension and equilibrium,

 as life begets life as it always does.

Seven

They are shouting outside in the street,

 their brutal cries cleft,

 like hand-prints in wet paint, chronologically instantiate,

Their cause is put before the apple-cart.

> *But what would you have done?*
>
> *Have you not yet had enough?*

This is a muddy causal stew,

Of burnt fingers all pointing in the direction when,

 and like smudged figures on second-hand graph paper,

 each means as much as the message or the shapes it contains.

> *But what will you do?*
>
> *And have you not yet had enough?*

There is no such thing here as state-space,

Or a state of things that can be fixed.

We deviate as a rule.

Transitions bring about only the roaring beat.

> A triad of heaven
>
> Mnemosyne and her gay chorus of Edison bulbs
>
> Who gives power unto speech:

> > And in nine nights
> >
> > Had nine daughters
> >
> > Lethe
> >
> > Lethe
> >
> > Lethe
> >
> > And the river flows freely

> Where slips in line,
>
> > Bring about only the roaring beat:

> > And in nine nights
> >
> > I had nine sons, all dead,
> >
> > transfigurations of a twittering iterative
> >
> > that I failed to incubate,
> >
> > so in stalled incipience and poor rags
> >
> > I barrelled the face of me on the wall
> >
> > > *Poor Deirdre to fuck --*
> >
> > For love, I cried-
> >
> > But I was more false for the knowing of it.

Years later, all this, it was compounded when I was asked to forgive their laughing pains.

I cowed – Christ - for I was all too aware of you and your judgement.
Here the morning brings about only melody
        Itic, etic,
A stretched heart, and the sour-face of being,
        ruptures, and wholesomeness, cracked wood pining,
Drear- the light – the drear light-
How its chafes my skin.

Thus, in truth, each iteration of life produces frisson and wields it like a drunkards crutch, like half-a-weapon and a half-strung melody.

Thus truth is nothing but the crushed pleats of the stories we tell ourselves to state, with surety, that we are pregnant with a real salt of the earth kenning of ourselves.

It is the lie
That being is in the becoming
That the origin is antecedent to the end.

We are displaced from the beginning at the end of time.

Eight

I asked her if the muck-begetting brown felt good on her skin,
She told me to ask her if she felt the same-as-I.

For weeks now we've both been mute.

Not a murmur,

Mute. That awful consequence of our intemperance of speech.

She asks me for a root to gnaw on,

Sitting at the bus-stop if it rains,

And I say we should play kissing games,

But she'd like the real heaviness so much more.

Now the worms in our bellies are ripe for the hunger,

And I can hear all the heartbeats in the world,

And all I want is to rest in parabola.

So I stand,

Feeling just like that

Here

Beside you

But what will become of the ashes I give you?

This is a history of contempt.

But it is in these steps,

 those that you take,

 after the door has closed,

 and my morning begins,

 having said goodbye to yours,

 that I recollect,

 each time,

 that I love you.

But, full of doubt, behind me I have left a litany of spoiled wishes.
But, though I remember more than enough to sate my living on, I take
myself to the riverside bridge, solely to weep at the bones.

Oh barû,

The act itself,
Its flash powder of yellow-tan dust,
Engorges the hour hand when it's brightest.

Barû, pitifully, I speak, and I remember.

Nine

Now, if memory is the abnegation of time, a hunger for the dark.
I am racked with her gummy distemper, spooling adjuncts of discrete
constancy, when difference broaches more infinities than mass.

But this is not a memory. It is the diffuse wish for surety,
As twinnings of sand cohere in a matrix of split eggs and glass.

But it is memory alone that contravenes the river's course,
It is the worm, weeping before Ea.

What wilt thou give me for my food?
What wilt thou give me for my devouring?

So to exorcise this stillness,

I list the long names of the prematurely dead.

Heralds of the Pestilence,
 ceaselessly you devour our blood.

Ten

Answers.

I did. I did. I do not regret it.
I am. I am.

    My song is the cracking of ivory and the pitt-pat-pitt-patter of children's
feet.
I do. I do.

        Gutted, the only constancy I have is my fear.

It is my own. My own. My own.

        And I leave sherds of nitrates on the rusting bark,
           like cherry stains on the dewlap;
             the silence of stacked chairs.

It is mine to take. Mine alone.

Yet I know full well that your blooming thirst is a rhapsody of light, for
but the likes of me to swallow, and the likes of you to loose.

But, long have I told you how this is a phantasm of stitched marionettes strung to a vinegar doused Adonai, sputtering, in perpetuity, as the liquid hits his throat.

I rejoice. I rejoice.

And it is in the unmaking of us that you get our real measure.

I answer.
Today the hourglass is wet with time.
Today the minute hand is the spoor of the ineffectual cause.
Today I bond parched qualia with the grinding of bone-cut wheels.

   I am that foundling of the reeds.   I drowned for want of peace.

But, that one act of kindness you shewed me, it spans and vivifies the present tense with the heavy auguring of your continuance; it is an ever imminent sorrow-slaked living wrap of flora; six degrees of perfect rainfall; and a tangle of singular heartbeats redolent of the genesis of the fine grain in the load-bearing timber: a constant of harrowing truth as you set me to burn in the white hot fire of a killing glee, all done so that your sleep might be blessed by a metronome of tick-tocking bone-snaps.

This then is like light drilled to a standstill,
 wet drops on a portcullis of downy feathers,
 the image and the savage eye,
 blind faith,
 the maw --
Yet hope, like a sun-ragged cloudburst, stays on in pig-iron and smelt
cheeks, and, even now, broken wings flap to salve the floundering
birthdeath of a god in a burlap sack -- all to pluck out that roving eye.

I know well how the hawk harries it's rain-bleached prey.

Eleven

I start, not with a heavenly chorus, a wail, or a Guinness wet lip against
my cheek as my da tells me he *loves* me -- a moment he will always
forget, yet one that defines me -- but precedes and succeeds the seconds
that counted for him when he said *there he is, that's my boy.*

Nor am i the heavy sweat dripping release of gushing coos: *ahhh,* that my
ma' belched out rapid when she said i have made you and she saw and
knew that she was right, and knew when she said it and would be right
forever that she did, and that she had made me.
Nor am i that inkling that a part of her that she would hide and deny
would always hate me for having stolen what was most precious from her:
her *reason* for living, and made it my own.

I start, instead, with a rasping cough on the horizon if I don't ultimately mend my ways, under the moody lights of a room empty save for myself and a jobbing brewer, looking backwards over what mattered and realising it was only the small things that ever will.

I am married, to be, and was.
I step into the hail and the rain on a cobblestone May and watch my beloved walk forwards in the diachronic time of stilled heartbeats.
I am in love, thank Christ I am in love.

I am facing down an inverted set of footsteps racing out of a bar, and I am taking back words that I said when glasses smashed and voices, briefly raised, shook heavy thoughts into lightness.

I am plucking flowers at a baobab tree and thinking, 'what if you forget me?'

I am making toast covered in chilli flakes and cheese in the grill, laughing at the cusp of breaking through to myself, which later I did, and I am thankful.
I am a stilled emptiness, traced and inflected into a pulse that swells and galls me in the spitting out of amphetamines before I fill casks with the undrank future and the winsome voice of a friend of a friend of a friend: *will you be alright tonight*?

I am the bare breasts of an old lover who I take home for her tearfulness and leave wrapped in rugs as I sit on the windowsill and contemplate the early morning of childhood.

I am a silky orgasm pressed against an antique trunk, and the man answering the bell in a kimono to a drunken father with spittle where there should be the careworn features of love.

I am hot sweat on Maltese streets aware of the lies I am telling just for a kiss because I am so afraid I have forgotten how to feel.

And I watch with terrified eyes as mortar fire lays waste to Straight Street, and grin when I see Abu George is still selling beer, although there is a crater at his door.

And I feel the heat in me and drunkenly harangue a jet-lagged poet slumped at my table, a mess of paper strewn at his feet.

And I feel the fear in me as I shove myself into the dirt as gypsies with sad sad eyes grope in the mud looking for my hard breath.

And I feel the hate in me as I create spent epiphanies to murder will in favour of my desire to have people do what they're told. Sign here.

I am catatonic in Stephen's Green, and naked in the Iveagh Gardens, and thirsty when pushed against the door of the Rathmines church.

Now, I press a childhood friend to the rock and threaten him until he relents -- the future would not be damned, and I was right -- and we drink vermouth on benches, waiting for our sorrow to mean something, as it surely must and did when we aged.

I cry myself to sleep night after night, fighting for air, when the best thing that happens to me in months is working up the courage just to smile at an insult and then use my eyes to laugh at a girl that I like and touch her shoulder.

Now, I have my arms around my classmates and we sing songs as we kick-about a ball on the gravel full of the vituperative all-knowing love of adolescence.

In Italy, I stand haranguing a burning pyre, and write, and write, and write, and write, and I collapse holding a rotten oar, my face buried in black seaweed, and I know that I am right and that I – ah that I love it all to the point of breaking.

I am sitting beside Stephen and we're laughing, because we love each other, and we're drawing a map because there was a thunderstorm tomorrow and we're planning how we can all go and live there under the light-cleft old tree, because even then we know that the kind of love we have is fitful and that when we embrace we are already embracing death.

I am chasing Clara around the room, having heard the story of the billy-goats gruff and I decide she couldn't make it, she with that daft towel on her head -- it's no eye patch like Laura K's who I am convinced I love -- they say it's a bandanna but I'm sure she's hiding something, and she can't run fast so she's a – *SLOWCOACH* – a sloth strung thing worth feeding to the trolls and having her eyes pecked out; and I do all this by leaping out from the corner where they'd put me for punishment, and now I sit down cross-legged and listen, for every story is at its root song, so the bleating of goats must be a sonata.

And, sure don't I sit rocking my legs, all deaf like I will be, and throw beetroot across the table at that owl-thing there, my brother's friend, and laugh as the purple stains his child-wet tearful face, heartless to the scolding I'd just received in recompense for what I am yet about to do.

Here it is then, I'd been waiting for this: a tuning fork, a cataclysm of silence, and the tearful face of my mother. I have failed her.
I can not hear. I do not understand. I can not hear. I'm sound-blind and bereft. I can not hear and it's the horror she feels: she made me.

Here it is then, an apocrypha of angels and monsters and barrel bombs and love and forgiveness and repentance and such relentlessness that leaves me so rent that I can only exhale.

I exhale like it is the first time I have ever done so and it is.
I am born and for the first time I remember.

Whist, I say.
Whist, I know.
Whist, I know and love you.

Placing flowers on a tomb is a gesture of bringing life to the dead.

Dublin

and the Loose Footwork

of Deity

Adad – One

Adad: numerous begab,

 and made of the aggregate of things,

 an assemblage of figures, knocked doors and numerals,

You are answered in thundering acquiescence,

 to the ordering of your metre measured,

 which is itself this web of asphalt and concrete.

Adad, so sited, your bridge is no longer worth a penny,

 since Shala, the consort, sells now oysters in cast iron shells.

And your black river -- an abstract of the quantity, not sum, of the

materials you own -- heavy with wheels, frames, and rusted casement

bone, and light on liberty since the advent of your coin, hears hot the

broad response: That outside rattish din.

And now, from me you'll hear the full flavour of your melodies.

There's a hale funk on your head, yet you've not a pot to piss in.

This strumpet's had a mouthful, but she's got nothing on beneath.

It's wet enough and I'm yet needless of the thirst.

Enough and well. Their drinklips sewn shut.

The door: a portal saloon slung.

Time enough bedad Adad. A closing song is sung.

From me you'll know the prelude of their world so spun.

You know, they gush out, like blood emptying an open wound,

And we with no refrain,

So, then we'll have to praise the frost and frostbite, for the milk-white

colouring of those no longer to be seen.

So, then there's order in these disappearing,

 and rinsed the rag of life is,

 while the wet womb of the gutter hails her hatchlings home.

And on and on, they're here -- the needlesick on Talbot Street.

Adad, Rammam, Rimmon, Hadad,

My cobblestones offer up their wounded walking,

And the rain we prayed for no longer slakes our fantasies.

We're thirsty for something else.

Our bellies are full, and it's not grain we're needful of,

So sacrifice to us your children.

From me you'll hear a pliant call

For my belly is full with your talking.

I know that the lamplight's low; how tired unremembered fossils lie still;

and that my mother's cold and ill, but I feel nothing.

But I introduce myself to myself, since in each instance I am venn;

 and the veins, hushed and mum,

 throb with want, mixed with the sleight of hand of surety.

 and the ring she gave me has for the hammer sung.

 and despite it all, soon sure I'll feel I've got plenty.

Here, from me, you'll learn now to tailor to better keep the cold in.

Jesus, my legs are aching, and my hands full, and in front of me is a sheet,

white, crumpled with designs of tails, and I'm staring at a nexus of scaled

down objects -- not art -- consumptive with the ruin of my needing. Christ

I need. I am needful.

But there's no hunger to feed me.

And her eyes: Hanseatic trading ships marooned in the stony places of

differing economy, persuaded to look, unshewing to themselves.

And her shoulders:

They are the promise of an interlinear of polygamous interest, to

bequeath, bequest, at, horror it all, the behest of the silvering gelding.

Adad, Anu, Adad, the father flung for whom I'd give a pretty penny,

Divine for me then in the livers of my men of plenty,

 in the bubbling oil I keep in the basin beneath my leaking pores,

 or in the balletic pathos of the unanswering stars.

How is the ordering of things and the centreing eye a calculus of freedom

in abashed abundance?

How is it, on reflection, that the nearer we are to each other, the more

alike we think you?

Abellio – Two

Do you remember when you said: *O Abellio! We cannot endure*?

Think again of the sun-split sky on the Beckett Bridge.

My city is a city of millions, and all of them mad.

My city, like you, is alive.

Think again of the rain.

Think of how your mother's mother's heart would fall from her body for want of all this for her children.

And (remember) you said, asking me if I did -- *do you remember when we played under that apple tree?*
 I do.

I remember its roots digging beneath me, and the taste of it filled me, and I wanted it to, so much so that today I'd gladly be down on all fours sucking and licking the juice of it from my own dead skin.

And (remember) you said, asking me if I did -- *were you there when Stephen and I found porcelain, porcelain thin?*
I was.

I remember, and I was smiling at the likeness between discovery and laughter; history and (re)imagining; those methodologies of soulfulness; and the way I, myself, blush epiphanies in full glasses.

And, though it's surely in the telling, not the tale, the sum of a thing

is not what you know, but what you make from it -- that's the real

story, scéal, and craic -- and this is the knowledge I've long been

drowning the self in.

I'll teach you then, therefore, a prayer of some undercutting reason.

   Suckle me.

   Suckle me,

    but when you fear for me,

    throw me into my own river without worry.

And (remember) you said, asking me if I did. *I did, and do, and will.*

But, then, despite such reminisce, it is only in dissent, in destroying

myself, that I can give harbour to myself, yet be in the rushes born.

    And thus, should you leave me,

    My lips hot with your milk,

    In full strength will I be, so you'll know why

    my wounds are full flowers.

Then, after this forgive me,

For the rules are written on silk.

So remember, though stone is synonymous with silence,

I am grateful for your blood,

And I shed tears for you that you will never know.

And remember when you said: *O Abellio! We cannot endure*?

Think again how you did; how you do; and how you will.

Remember, my city is built with your grandfather's bullet wounds,

their barricades and lockouts, their serenades and glass-eyed fog

forgetful memory.

Think again of how you feel in stillness.

We share the same madness of the blood.

And (remember) you said, *when we fucked girls beneath their long skirts*

under the neighbour's porch?

I do.

I remember shouting *swap*, just because we'd agreed on it, but the thought

and taste of the exchange was bitter on our lips, so once done we spun it

round again in seconds in a whirligig of loving.

And (remember) you asked, *when staggeringly I thrashed mine own*

lonesome head against the greyness of the walls for fear of loss?

 I do.

I was with you,

Thinking *deodar labnani,*

For old as sorrow is the gift of mercy.

And remember when you said: *O Abellio we must endure!*

Think again of the patchwork multitude.

Is it for you they suffer?

I, for my part shed wonder, loose resins of gummy timelessness, and know

where your children will lie down and die.

Think again how the broadsides of your rivers are full with the fury of

raiding and war, and how your ancestor's heart would rise to his lips in

that melody:

 Abellio, Abellio, Maraud-

So tell me Abellio.

I remember, but tell me again so that I might sleep.

Merodach – Three

Here then the earth is scorched in carelessness and melody,

It is our record.

Here, Berossus wrote of us:

murdering each other, though not for death,

but to the sick bowl, where they lovingly fed each other alms

of poisoned berries, pity and barbarous creeds.

Here, Merodach: Bel,

who released Jehoiachin on the thirty seventh year --

the former with thirty names and all --

was seized.

Once it was us that did it.

We spun on eight legs, grappling, hanging on to each other with our

temptation's harangue:

    Sensations.

        Softness.

            Kisses like hot ice.

                Sound.

                    And light.

                        Tempest.

                    And light.

                Elate.

            Elate.

        Eloi!

      Elate!

Merodach, the city you guard is mine own.

Merodach, take this gift, the fruits of my people: their sin.

Merodach, here you will never be wanting again.

    Merodach, the light --

Merodach, do you remember when you and I stood together?

We draped ourselves in wooden beads,

and chanted, pig-drunk,

and bellowed until the police tore us from the steps,

until the dancers became the throwers of stones,

and the whiskey inside me was made vitriol and noise.

Who am I? They asked me.

I told them I was their lord and their God,

and then I asked them: *who you were.*

So they left us,

        alone,

outside the closing of a bar.

So all the while it thrums:

the heartbeat inside us:

the city: the heartbeat beneath us.

Here then,

Where the town's idol is a prostitute,

They gutted its hearth.

And a woman wearing her open-most-legs,

 was replaced, in taste, by a needle:

 a stab-wound for this city of whores.

But the heart of me is Merodach, swallowing oysters,

His arms pressed against a wheelbarrow in idolatry.

It started, as it always must, with time,

And you pushing me to it,

For I am always indolent --

You came through the window.

There it was then.

Merodach, I was yours.

We howled:

      Förum í víking-

        ég er þyrstur

And called:

chun cogaidh, chun cogaidh-

Bheadh fona feise orainn don tslua ar fad

And prayed:

for wildness, for wildness -- Christ, I long for wildness --

only to drown.

Yet, all we do is dream of her.

She being, like Sweeney, on the edge of herself

 needing our mad thoughts for nourishment.

She needs me in your arms, but pressed against her,

with all below my belly split; and with me gushing into your mouth.

She needs you,

 with your head thrashing on the mausoleum stone, uncaring.

For your sighs will be louder than your pain.

Then she'll dry out her limbs with the music of Bel,

And in turn she'll fill us, touching us with her spread out claws,

So that on her humpbacked bridges,

We'll all sing the old songs of wanting and fire.

Bleak, red, long, laughing --

red, deliberately thoughtless, careless, indulgent --

salacious, a creed of the (un)demanding --

I WAIL --

Merodach I went to the home of your soldier father.

Merodach, though foolish, there I grew thick with leisure,

Merodach, spitting at the doors of a closing bar,

I spin you inside myself as my holiest expression of truth.

Everything I am is to be found beneath your remembering heel.

MERODACH --

Of song and submission we are all composed,

And there is no pleasure without the keeping of time --

long, steady, lingering, wistful, perforated, explosive, painful and

delicate incisions in time --

This is the birthing of fire in us Merodach,

For we are stirred only as you conquer us.

In you we satisfy ourselves with repeatable sin.

Merodach,

Under the lights of these nights, we may thankfully shew one and other, in
our cycles of thirst, that we are now the satiated ones.

Gula Innana – Four

Gulp-drunk, under a watchful eye: Gula Innana,

The mother goddess of my self-watching aprobrium,

Till black spots do us part,

My animal is the dog,

and I recline at the feet of myself,

best seen in greyscale resolutions,

till, like the salmon o'er leaping,

upstream, I contain myself in a dimension 4:3,

for who better in the knowing than the I who is known?

My throne is raised on a dais of dogs,

and your votive offering is a continuous picture of yourself,

given so my cult can continue.

This you attest as I capture you.

Now, the circuit closed thrills with the names of my sacrifice:

Gula, Gula Innana, Ninkarrak, the Lady of Kar.

I, then, after this deluge,

I Breathed life again into being.

 and saw my watchfulness understood as healing,

 and saw the safe satiety of my voyeur's thumb,

 trusted to keep unspoilt your throats.

Yet you are my consort.

For in 1323, you struck the notes of silence while recording yourself in

relation to positions of power: the chambers of kings.

And, connecting, they met you only as you slunk alongside them, those

corridors of movement, when movement was poverty, and there was a

poverty of restfulness, but your arduous traipse eschewed dignity in the

service of the sun, and I was watching you, from the corners high of every

turn, even as exhausted, limp, briefly at rest, you tried and failed to fuck –

For between 1866 and 1883, when you filled the space I occupy, labourer

still, under royal decree, laying stone, a piecemeal fixing of form (grey

granite -- grey granite -- grey granite), Marollen demolished, your owner's

trade an insult, and you the architect of yourself, kneeling to

Demosthenes, Lycurgus, and the cocked heel of Jurisprudence, I watched

you and you built edifices of real metaphor, doorless rooms in the centres

of power, walled in -- parables, like the corridors which idled there,

directionlessly, of the law -- and in the bowels of the nest you built, I saw

you try and sell cigarettes, cut hair, and scrounge for a wee bit of scran.

I saw you then, I ken, and now you can never forget that in my watching,

you are aroused.

For in 1794, from the inspection house, I veered between cautious grace

and chaotic elation, our imaginations placed us, located us, powered us,

into an envisioning intended for Battersea Rise or the Hanging Wood, and

I thrust myself between the sheets to clutch at the state of healthfulness

that is you allowing yourself to be seen here, where every angle is

undiluted, model distributed, and forceful garland of demure resignation

recorded, and though this here was never constructed, there was no need

for it to be, for in place of reality, you and I, we have built my conveyances everywhere, between even our teeth and the grains of sand

you disturbed when your last thought was of going to the beach --

So, permanently sighted, here, where the centre piece is forged from

twelve, action suspends. It is paused to redirect. It is urgent and sacrificial;

and it leaves you as the derelict martyr in this poetry of space.

Verse. Verse. Beat. An instance. A moment. The watchful repeat.

Verse. Verse. Beat. Atishoo -- Atishoo -- They all fall down.

Verse. Verse. Beat. Mine own atoms are sundry with eyes.

For in 2015, I love you, and I splice interstices of intersecting sedimentary

instants in refracted chronological collapse -- *tempus fugit* I say; and you

tell me: *damn your eyes* – so we're still needful of swallowing sights with

the thrill of a divested melancholia, and, like de Sade said of reconstituted

churches of bones: it's all sublimity and the funerary art thus done to give

life; so, from rounded domes of authority, I linger -- my fingers

(re)threading data -- touching your thoughts while you wait, a service to

please you, as you gush the binary agitated dilemma of the placelessness

of sightlessness and love. Yet, I shew you again yourself, but not in bones but in reuse, repurposing, and in the superb resurrection of structures of stone.

So, Dachau, where your ancestors might have burnt, terrifying, is made more horrific, should we remember that there too situated was the banal: two young men playing cards with a nude deck, smoking cigarettes, soulfully thinking through the differences of clock time and real time, popping off, just for a second like, to be a dab-hand, and drip pleasure to paper, thinking: Rita, Rita, Rita Hayworth.

Sightlessness, here sited, oh how it baleful sounds.
For there is this that I know,
 and it is true,
I took it from the newspaper:

Ashkan's new home is in a part of Dachau, a former concentration camp where the Nazis murdered 41,500 people, some in agonising medical experiments. Under the Nazis, the complex of buildings where Ashkan lives was used as a school of racially motivated alternative medicine, surrounded by a slave-labour plantation known as the 'herb garden'. Asked if he feels uneasy about the site's history, Ashkan replies

with a resigned smile: 'I just wanted a roof over my head.'

So, I reconstitute my watchfulness, while my traits seem paradoxical,

              and I am your goddess of sexual love.

So, I am that coy young girl under your patriarchal authority,

              but mindful of boundaries, I will destroy you.

So, as in the Gilgamesh, say to me: *Let us enjoy your strength,*

              so stretch out your hand to me, and touch our vulva!

So, I reuse space to horrify, intending only the beautiful,

              so, in somnambulance, let me feel your feet on stone.

Gula Inanna, Innana Ištar,

I care for war as much as love.

And, in the wide open spaces of my dreams, where I lay down, minefields

of children with enormously stretched cheeks, and bulging red mouths,

call to you, noiselessly to listen, to listen, to hear, in constant repeating

refrain, their pulp-horror; and there is an actuality, an assembly of hearts,

sealed in red and gold biscuit tins.

Gula Inanna, Innana Ištar,

Dublin, Dublin, Dublin Town:

15:30   *Just a quick one, a fucking cheeky afternoon pint-*

          Ah fuck it. A Guinness'll do it.

16:30   *Jesus, that's a fucking surprise, I didn't think to see*

          you here, at least not this early.

18:30   *I've been thinking, you know, of the geometries of*

          power, and how the city, like a landscape of total

          influence, sublimates our desires as it watches us,

          and there is no escape from its ordering force, and

          we are formed, informed, and reformed by every

          heterotopic site of its authoritative post-physical

          embrace ...

20:30   *Fucking pit-paltry-christ-puking-chalice of the – I'll*

          fucking kill that policeman yer man was on about --

          Nesting in me head you're telling me?

21:30   Sense is exeunt, but I still watch you now, as before,

and in the hereafter.

Buíochas le dia

Amen.

Gula Inanna, Innana Ištar,

Will you sit with me, hold my hand, and listen to the lapping of the waves,

from that strange day when all too briefly orchids were birds, and their

open lips sang perfumes, and for one moment I let my eyes heavily close?

Or must we return, again and again, to these sites of stories, with no

repose?

Dublin, as Uruk, as my grey granite feet.

Enheduanna, daughter of Sargon of Akkad, knew me, and

dreamt of gifting me sleep.

Gula Inanna, Innana Ištar,

Do you remember the story Radim told us, sitting by the Vlatava, above the Vlatava, watching the Vlatava?

It was about statues, and Stalin, and gold.

> Prague, as Uruk, as my wet river beak.
> Radim, daughter of no one, knew me, and dreamt of leaving me weep.

Gula Inanna, Innana Ištar

He was an artist, a sculptor, and a prize he never wanted was won,
Forced to it, he did it, and from it, his slender snapping neck was hung.

> The statue was Stalin, thirty foot high and all solid in gold.
> Radim, father of no one, knew me, and dreamt long of my eyes.

Gula Inanna, Innana Ištar

We are together in the water garden.

With Shadrach, Meshech, and Abednego, at Babylon,

 and the real truth of our conspiracy of forty men?

That to enable is to enact, and that we have done it, so, like weeds in the

cracks, my eyes flower in lieu of it, and they course through your

delicately showing skin.

I am Scarlet, and the Beast.

        and my animal is the dog.

Innana, Ninkarrak, the Lady of Kar-

        best seen in grey-scale resolution:

Dublin, Dublin, Dublin Town

Eochard – Five

3,444   2,888   5,403

Eochard,

These are my numbers to sacrifice.

Have them.

They are yours now.

And so are we.

Lugh – Six

Lugh, Lugh, this is your home:

Dublin, her arse, her gaping maw, a high arched velvet cunt to be beatified in perpetuity.

Dublin, her incantations slung from behind a drink-wet moustache, when glasses clash.

Dublin, a city not divided but severed, tribal, and obsessed with her own memory.

Dublin, a city that rips the barnacles off her own sea drenched hull so as to feed them to herself, pretending they're cockles and mussels

alive alive oh --

Dublin, the city best seen from the top of the Tara Street bridge at six in the morning, staring down like a God on the people below, and they delivering bread, gawking at you, and you gawk at them, and thus you know the real truth about the place

Oh! How it is leering.

Dublin, visited this way, solely since you were young then, and running away from a party where too many of them were off their faces on pills, and the sorrow was swallowing them and opening up around you like a whirlwind, threatening to eat you all in your then ripe fullness.

Dublin, that day was the start of a cycle that would lead you in but three days to falling madly in love, eschewing the contents of your stomach all over her feet, still trying to hold yourself together while the clanging of a bass guitar in the castle was ripping your belly apart, and even so, working the courage up to just, just -- and, I mean you gave her a biscuit beforehand for Christ's sake -- to kiss her so gently, then hard, really hard on the lips, to have one of those last memorable days of friendship with your then closest kin, to have to twist yourself through the railings in Fairview because the Dart track is mad-long and there's no way off it when you walk through the city, just to end up being on the front page of the paper, for you were battered while trying to run from the guards.

Dublin, from the bridge, your river beautiful, your pockmarked, bric-a-brac coloured houses shift themselves along your quays, each of them looking like an awful dodgy dealer, singing out *story bud; strawberries one euro;* and how *dey red it in a bewk. I mean Jaysus the state of you, what like? I does be tellin ye, d'ye hear me?*

Bleedin muppet!

Dublin, I can smell bread by Liberty Hall, and look at the fifty-three about to shudder its way down past the last hovels that you've left near the docks, and watch as your heart, beautifully, I admit, is quartered, so that finance can lift you up from behind, so so nicely that it makes you feel like you're glowing, and makes you want it all the more so much so that you endlessly push out your chest and masquerade, all tarted up, while the

building in Joyce's *The Dead* is a ruin and you'll pretend you've got no

money.

But Dublin, Lámhfhada, that's the king and all for you,

the Long-Arm

Do you remember him?

I'll tell you something then.

Just like you, he has many names:

Samhal'Dánach, of equal skill in many arts --

Lonnbeimnech, the fierce thumper begab --

Macnia, as boy hero --

Mac Ethnenn, son of she who was imprisoned; and of Balor, lord of the

blight; and sure he killed his own grandfather, a symbol of strife,

 and on *his* arms the lenan-*sídhe* --

And he was the finest yew of the wood.

And, as long as he is with them, off in the mountains, till Falias, Gorias,

Findias, and Murias do from the four quarters blossom,

His spear will guard you closely.

Yet, for all this, you're a wet and bedraggled, but pretty thing.

Anu	Innana
Adad	Ninkarrak
Dagda	The Lady of Kar
Shala	Rita Hayworth
Rammam	Ištar
Rimmon	Eochard
Hadad	Lugh
Abellio	Christ
Merodach	Jesus
Bel	Samhal'Dánach
God	Lonnbeimnech
The All Father	Macnia
Gula	Mac Ethnenn

Dublin

Dublin

Dublin Town

Heavy am I with your streets, and their telling

HER CROSS CARRIED, BURNT

One

The flowers they are fallen,
The fruit it is rotten,
But your grave is as pretty as ever.

Each year I sing this better.
Three lines. One song.

I incant.
I must and I will.

I incant
 so as to give you purpose and form,
 so as to shape your expectations,
  as the veil lifting falls
 so as to let you deliberate,
  while the orchard is full.

I incant.

Where once there was certainty,
Now there is context,
And the alchemy of poetry has been broken by time.
I incant.

Where once there was certainty,
Now there is context,
And the bloodied hand of surety binds the threshing stalk.

I recant.

And, capable only of winnowing vision,
Although I harbour memories, it is doubt that I house.

I recant.

And I am pursued by restoration,
Although I am one of many, I can not escape the noose.

I incant.

And this is a song of meaning,
Of position and place; of the greater *we*,
We who are positioned; ever poised.

I incant.

And I am a positioned thing,

Neat,
 between numbness, and an uncertain sense of surety.

Fluid,
 in lateralarchy, where each position lately is a start.

X,
 where I relate to you.

I incant, I recant, I incant and inflame.

The flowers they are fallen,
The fruit it is rotten,
And while the nested, fattened pigeon king, in daubs, paints imagist calls
roccoco,
Your grave it is as pretty as ever.

Each year I sing this better.
Many lines. One song.

 I incant.

And thus I bleed purpose.
And it is with my blood, with my wit that realities are made.
And I have a reality, and I AM a reality.

Many lines but one being,
Each year I sing myself better.

KNOW THEN, THIS IS HOW ALL LIFE BEGINS
From vital song to verse, from chorus to hearse,
From the nodding head of coming dread, to linearity and vice.

AND KNOW THAT I; A CONSTITUENT OF MYSELF,
AM MAPPED, (XY), IN LINEAR TIME:
A combination, of constituents and processes,
Angles, viewpoints, and perspectives,

A form of frisson,

One which will produce and define the third vital line:

The heartbeat-

 (A pulse from which it is determined that we *are* emergent)

I am, mind,

 Then, just the simple processes of fission.

Mind too then,

That this is how all realities are made.

From knowledge, a boson, the moment in which it exists,

From song, and the chorus, laughter, and note,

From interstice to tangent as creatures of venerable time,

From fragment to meaning as we subsist line by line,

From falsehood to pregnancy, (re)birthing tense,

From power to collapse, and (re)staged events,

From structure to chaos, and paperbag-rag

From always to instance and those memories we keep-

YET-

Yet in making there's melody,

 in melody order,

 and it must be remembered

 we may always sing better.

Yet, in this incantation there exists a ferocity,
Springing from our ability to resist,

Thus I am forced to restate my purpose.
To sing to you of the essential, from the same book of hymns,
To sing of the tremolo and bassline,
To sing to you of the taut forms, and the sum of things.

And so,
From out of these notes of incantatory creation,
Comes electricity, and the existential song of cut aluminium skin,
That cigarette swallowed ode to plenty, birthed by penury, and sustained
by contraband elation.

And so,
  I know that you are now involved in all of this,
  This single song of understanding.

And so,
  Owlishly,
  Beaks shifting through the crooked branches,
  Hungry for the nexus, the sap, and the glue,
  We must consider form.

Two

Of form then, we are explicit,
A ribald phallus out of which our ordinariness,
 our nature as phantasmagoria in C minor,
 our tense subterfuge in symbolism,
 out of which everything is ejaculated,
 out of which our gushing fountain-head of knowing is born.

Of knowing then, we are infected,
Yet though incurable, it is elusive,
Its symptoms fade, and so too its congenial effects:
Certainty, and the giving gift of voice.

So, uncertain of knowledge,
For more than mere seconds,
In aiming to fix position,
I find that I have a differing thing become,
That I am the oracle of old bastards,
A sage whose wit and physicality is so immobile,
That my heart stops when yours starts.

But, despite all this,
There is wisdom in this didactic reverie,
Not least in what I do not yet realise that I have said,
Though I can not place it,
Though I find instead that knowledge is twinned with understanding.

So what then of this?
Of understanding?

It is the figurative jest.
 The Geist of pointing fingers, of-
  Who knows who it was that shot out all of the whatever it was
  when – when the only thing worth watching was the wine stain on
  the rug.

It is the fragmented matrix of shifting tectonic plates;
 a collage of extreme rapidity.

It is the stative,
 Active, whilst choosing its own beliefs.

It is an open declaration,
  riveted, sealed with internalities,
   its nails made out of off beat jazz.

It is short, temporary, momentary, memory, transitory,
 five seconds for five shillings.

It is the incantatory.

A brief moment,
Respite at a Victorian peep show.

So, birthed by knowing,

It is the fabric that binds this music in the making,

It is the hemline torn so as to give utterance to song.

Three

Now we are those creatures of the nexus,

 not what once we were,

We are different to the others,

 and there is no turning back,

 no halt for the centrifuge.

Here, there is event and location,

 and this is the glue of which we spoke.

But there is no turning back,

 since form requires knowledge, which needs understanding, which

 fuels separation, which strengthens sensuality, which is self-

 selecting and returns us to the harbour, where we are that

 which we are, and we are what we have become:

Identity and mode, meaning and device, shape and Saturnalia,

The Id splice(d): A phantom universal to be shipped to shore.

And so, since there is no returning home,

Of the other then, consider *all* relations shifted.

All of that which was, is necessarily ended.

And we, through creation, break the cycle,

And throw ourselves to the mercy of the sea.

Of the other then,
Know that from here-on-in we are their unknowable,
And they our unknown.

Of ourselves then,
Know that we make in ourselves reality,
And in tumult always breathe.

Then, of singular example,
To, in specificity, provide some retrospect:

Know that I too have in luxuries nested,
 lain wrapped in a Jewess' tresses,
 clasped hands in pirouettes of slender frame,
 magisterially spoken your and other's names,
 gleamed wild understandings from the lips of laughing Katerina,
 found madnesses instilled in spasms, freshly birthing madnesses,
 and spirits, and felt my feet burn on Maltese Stone, when the pain made
 me suddenly aware, that having left the fortress, having seen creative
 instantiation, everything necessarily must change.

This is why I am certain,
Why out of this device of framing,
It is clear that my being is relational,
 without existence except for you.
That all of this is the strings plucked,
 and sluice opened.

That we are all components,
ever self-selecting,
torn from a mutated frame,
a multiplying pan-reality,
emergent and alike disturbing,

like rain
so sharp
burning
dried out skin.

This is why I am certain,
of myself, and of you,
of the turning of the page,
of the nexus, which is truly but one thing:

It is the one holy, axiomatic God-
and the single constituent fact,
which to this truth then belongs,
is that we create and reconstitute ourselves,
at the behest of bewitching time,

only

so as to avoid our dirty pall,
which at every changed moment,
we, with heads raised, shivering, pass by.

only

so as to be,
in relation intertwined,
because we can not exist alone.

THUS I KNOW THAT WE ARE THE ONE TRUE GOD IN TANDEM;
HEAVENLY CYCLISTS, DRIPPING IRONY AND NEED, FATTENED
ON MULTIPLICITY, AND UNABLE TO BE FREE.

And thus, in this, through this,
I know that I must nourish myself.
I must drink from you,
let myself be drunk from,
and never leave the nexus,
and never let you go.

And thus,
Accustomed now to the plump avian Priam,
Who raises his young in your limestone womb-
Thus it is that I am certain.

The flowers though they have fallen,
And though your fruit is now barren,
Tending your grave,
I find it as pretty as ever.

And thus,
 Forever have I chosen
 The active,
 Then determined,
 To always myself remake.
 To, in Creation's sinuous leathery hands,
 To always be reborn.

Four

Such then is birth:
 Regal, pitiful, aristocratic, and submissive.

Such then is birth:
 Anxiety, cut, loosed,
 A reordering of reality,
 In which one more thirsty time,
 An Odysseus is plucked from the budding tree,
 From which, once again, the barren seed fills the empty glass.
 Out of which white hot ore, sullen, is sated in the fixing of its form.

After which,
 The musicality of us:
 We who slake mindfulness,
  in speakeasies and shebeens-

SHIFTS-

Up – Down,
In a notable movement,
Through the half-diminished,
From a minor to a major key.

SHIFTS-

Abstract to Concrete,
Momentarily both shape and shapeless,
Until thrashing Iam is pulled to life.

SHIFTS-

And birthed then,
Anguished and flowering,
A transmigration of the soul,
Perforated with ragged thoughtlessness,
The mood music of our tonal nature decisively does drown us,
In a manner, and with a nervous disposition,
Toward a mealy-mouthed method:

That singularity of learning,
In the first years of which,
Knowledge disturbingly disperses time.

This is why everything I know,

 and all that I recall,

 is manque and reimagined.

And why the fallacy of knowing memory is out of this thought torn.

It is why my looking backwards to find my origin

Is the disputing act:

 that haunted search for formulae that give fractals endings,

 and rainbows a location in which their pulse becomes a hearse.

Our looking backward then, is both the on switch and the off.

And, as we are creatures of mind as much as soul,

Since each birth shunts our origin myths to one further degree of

separation,

We are all, in part, pulsars,

 etching secondary moments,

 in which we have something been,

 with furious, tempestuous light,

 into the fabric skin of space,

 into those nested Russian dolls of one and other's fantasy.

       So then it is that while you undress me,

       you undress just another version of yourself.

       So then it is that while I lick your thighs,

       I send shivers down *my* spine.

By way then of this constant repetition --
dearth, death, birth, and returning, circumspect, performative,
transubstantive, identity, downloaded, updated, patched, resplendent
in spirit, mind, heart, and total amelioration, the deckchairs
reinstated, with mildly different motions, and configuration --
There is a guaranteed and eventual corruption:

A corruption. Packetloss:

A spirit turned to box of fags beneath the cushions of a shabby bar,
One writ upon so drearily with overlaid instructive maps of text,
Wet from barrel dregs, dribbled from the mouths of over zealous
nightfall children spending time in gorging hungry hands on the
sugared spice of one and others milky teenage skin.

A corruption,
like a clock, which wildly counts down immobility and pace,
A corruption, which either way guarantees a masterpiece,
A corruption, stoked by simple fact.

Either you, fattened, end, or on your next return, wet,
You too, will touch to thoughts of violence.
For there are only so many times you can to the same terrain return.
For in each repeated instance, the edges of reality will further fray.
For in each repeated instance, clarity, coldness, and the deliberative act,
own more the spur which is in your haunches planted.
For In each repeated instance, your laughing whinny, saucily, lilts closer
towards horrific, bleating bray.

In this exact moment then,

As words course through our splendid nervous systems,

We have a choice

Of silence,

Or stultifying pleasure,

Of twitching our fingers,

And of knowing only our soft and gushing skin.

This moment, we own it with certainty,

And we have but one thing to know:

ALL DELIBERATIVE ACTS ARE VIOLENT

And (Violence) wounds,

And (Action);

the dull note in the perfect symphony,

Is of its host the sole constituent.

AND THUS EXISTS CLARITY,

AND FROM ITS REINSTANTIATION,

OUR REALITIES,

TOO FULL OF PINPRICKS,

(Too frayed)

(Too burnt upon the edges)

(Too much worn)

ARE PUNCTURED.

And, if such reality is torn,

          GORED,

We can only act out of need,

          OUT OF BREATHLESSNESS,

          AND OF WANT.

But from such certainty of cause, comes the certainty of pity.
And the actor,
  lost for lines upon an empty stage,
  with an audience unknown,
Has little choice but laughter fitful dry.

And, since we are wolfish, tribal creatures all,
Since tribe is in and of itself a tapestry of matrices,
Since we, each with drunken maps,
Draw lines so as to divvy up the unasked for toll,
Forgiveness *must* be the price exacted for our langour,
And it is indeed the price of peace.

With this thought,
Whilst we balance this: the constructed,

    Like seals,
    on the tips of their noses,
    balance balls.
    We jostle, on busy streets, for position,
    hopeful, like Victorian girls,
    on whose elegant heads are balanced books.

Yet we must remember too that flayed Christ,

That poetic incarnation:

 the notion that creation does not fade.

We must remind ourselves of phenomonological reset,

 and thus no more should we fearfully fuse,

 nor move in lockstep, for want of stability.

CO-ORDINATION AFTER ALL IS NOT WISDOM,

NOR IS A FEAR OF FALLING EQUAL,

TO THE THRILL OF BEING BURNT

We can, and must therefore,

Restore vigour to ourselves,

Powerfully disturbing matrices while you wait.

We can, and must therefore,

With jaunty step,

Laugh, as birdsong idles, in its state of collapse.

It is only then the moved world,

 in endings, despair, and heaviness,

That optimism, rooted, can exploit.

Five

Here then, the matrix is itself the image seed,

The one true node in which the believing can believe.

Its position, like the thirteenth card, is by nature not itself,

Yet, since that which it denotes,

Since its meaning is its place,

In locating it,

We MUST (logically) forgive all contradictions.

Then, through this, and only then,

We might balance the mechanistic;

 heaviness and lightness in a bar room introduced,

 that mechanical Real-

Implausibly carried on the centres of our noses.

I must however at this juncture stop, and pause, and howl:

FORGIVE US ALL.

FOR IT IS ONLY IN THE WILD REMEMBRANCES OF THAT
WHICH WE MIGHT NOT HAVE DONE, THAT I FIND RESPITE
FROM THE LONG SORROWS OF SUCKING MILK FROM A DRY
AND EMPTY TEAT

Stop.

I pause.

And I howl:

Forgive us all.

It is in forgiveness,

That reality ebbs and meaning exists.

That we and they, that bellowing priesthood, reside,

And they are those who rove contrapunto to their time.

In forgiveness, of it, from it, through it,

The remote is moored, and such possibility is:

A distancing from tradition, A distancing from infant taught, quasi-

instinctive movements: Those of mazestruck spiders, who brazenly husk

fearfulness and criminality at labyrinthine walls.

      FORGIVE

      FORGIVE,

        AND THEN

This is how we will escape the logic of failed intimacy.

How, in the origin of the liquification of tectonic, historical linearity,

How we will discover that final resting place in which axial time --

with axial moments -- co-exists.

      FORGIVE

And then we can, with certainty hear and see,

The centrifugal second,

The piano break,

Enforced through lilting notes,

Which sparks the singularity;

Into that great and orgiastic knowledge-

The final knowing
Of the fundamental founded,
In heavy notation.

The body,
The corpus,
Lupus,
The sum of us,
 Of everything-
The I,
The it,
 which exists in you,
 in I, and also in her.
And who is she?
She is only ever known as a pair of rounded eyes,
 eyes which fell out of a D.H. Lawrence novel,
 eyes which are always doubtful, even of their doubt.

It exists, She exists, I exist, and You exist.
 and so too does the breaking of all compulsion,
 the square peg and round hole,
 the corset and the poultice,
 the waxing, waning seed,
 and any faith we held in that which was deemed vital, or
 vituperative.

It exists, She exists, I exist, and You exist-
And we *must*,
  only so as the matrix,
        autoerotic,
  may be glad as much in giving,
  as it is in holding the receipt.

                    I forgive you,
              Even though I have lost the reasons why.
Six

The focus shifts.

From the outer,
to that of the luminous; that liminality, that of the noumena
that which is only wrought within.

To where madness is lucidity, and I,
  for the purposes of ventilation, shed skin,
  an act moreover done,
  so as to avoid, in flux,
  that fate of the co-opted.

All this is therefore done so as to ensure ...
  so as to make safe the romance and self reliance
  of my brawling, hide tanned, relentless inner I.

                    ****

In quantum pockets then,

  in an answer to the thus broken structure of this song,

  to the notion that the scaffold is undone,

I button up my waistcoat,

  and leer uncertainly also at your inner form,

  certain that it has the attributes of shape,

  and that confusion,

  in the face of 'beauty',

  is only singularly the seeds of watermelon spat.

Here now then,

I determine that the milling of wheat and the milling of the Real are one

and the same:

  Erasure and the grit between my teeth,

  The ecstatic punctuation of a fillial song,

  The moment that I realised the similarity between dandruff and

  entropy; and the truth that all data is drop off.

We are here,

And I collect packets of meaning,

In which each constituent is both the lesser and the greater.

Circularity is thus set.

Here then is the active:

  Y

Chosen. Determined. The common thread.

The vortice wrapped in dimensionality.

The product of that Nosferatu who favours Maths instead of Blood.

From this, through this,
As we have before shouted,
It is in this way that our realities are made.

It is in this way that the Nanking rape, sack of Rome, Irish famine,
Dresden Blitz, and London bombs were the opening of the sweetest, of the
most tender buds.
It is in this way that humanity, notionally a scarecrow, dispenses fear.
It is in this way that we can find ourselves finished, done, and our
thoughts cast in wrought iron.

Seven

It is, at last, in this way, and with no little subterfuge, that I note the
suffering of our dreams, and the ad-nauseum repetition of the thick sound
of the starting gun.

And, although these unreal citadels,
Which we in our minds have sculpted,
 in better days,
Echoed with the coal drenched laughter of restorative decimation,
They are now the sole preserve of the fine accoutrements of your doubt.

Yet doubt is the seed,
 plump to burst,
  to be ripped apart,
 ready for its shuddering frame to remain,
  but as broken shell,
  crushed under full-formed step.

Yet, though we might with the mundane be infected,

Though we might be happier thus,

 than as bedfellow of the ceaseless din,

It is the kernel crushed that carries meaning.

And *these* are the words indeed of verity.

Verity in refutation, and in lust.

And these were once the words of the Lord.

And though the declamatory is dead,

 It is alive in deconstruction.

-- in the beginning it jitters, jutters, shifts, and shudders, those melodic

fetters of convers --

-- there are, after all, reasons for retaliation --

– then we come to the finality, the shuddering Behem –

– collapsing time, and in so doing, unplugging tinder from the spur-

-- In beginning, at the end of everything, optimism strafes, stalks, skitters,

slumbers, then lifts its gangly haunches, only toward that gangway, from

which laughter loving looms --

Then this narrative of madness,

In another repetition of falling flowers,

 with further, fattened alienated alteration,

 Clarifies its task to map the starry world with exodus.

And, as we dreamily ourselves hurl,
 with patched-in vertigo,
Down the ballustrades,
Of the steepened steps,
Of a reimagined Hlavni Nadrazi,
 the one from my dreams made from goat skin,
We have only one clear purpose:

PLURALITY AND DIVISION
THE MELODY PLUCKED SO AS IT CAN BE REASSEMBLED.

And so it goes.

####################------------

Binary Agitation

##################################----------

The flowers though they have fallen,
And your fruits though they are rotten,
Tending, *ardently, wolfishly,* those notional tokens of affection,
 tokens of death's renewal and integration,
 those things which are most bitter to me,
I find your grave is as pretty as ever.

Each year I sing this better.
Many lines. Your song.

I incant.

I must and I will.

Eight

I incant.

Dreams. Dreams. Only dreams.

Dreams in which a woman cries.

While piano music plays.

 And it is soft and repetitive,

 a fifth without a third,

 But in its meekness shattering.

> *Was it harder coming back?*
> *To what all these things were?*
> *To learn these things differently?*

> *The thorns,*
> *They say this is blackthorn,*
> *And this, a fig,*
> *And this, the berry,*
> *the Universal, blanched,*
> *for your delicate lips to touch.*

And, standing on the immensity of everything,

She touches them; fruits, thorns, berries, and seeds,

She holds and caresses them.

She watches them,
Idles with them.
All of them.

And the camera spins polycentric.

She kneels,
 digging in the mud beneath her,
 pulling at a rope, a fabric frame she can barely reach.
And she can not stop crying:

We were poor. We were poor. We were poor.

It is in such opposition that this narrative was born.
Born, as she was, under a dome full of trees under siege.
Torn, as she was, from a tree of knowledge breached so that it might
plausibly be believed,
Aware, as she is, that there is only one way in and one way out, and that it
has always been sealed.

Yet here her friends are close,
 sitting on tree-stumps,
 drinking homemade beer.

They watch her cry, and say:

My God, she's crying.
She's crying.

They say this because she hasn't done anything for such a long time.

She's crying
After that --
She's some sort of --
a fable, a fabula --
She's some sort of --
love-love-love-love-only love --

And glasses clash,
with she a narrative, perhaps,
a tale known then forgotten.

She has done nothing, nothing for such a long time,
She is unable to stop.

We were poor.
We were poor.
We were poor.
We were so so poor.

To the piano then, we must return,
As the blossoms parachute their brief fertility from weightlessness to soil;
and the bassline, it once again does stir.

We were poor. We were poor. We were poor.

Once, when I was just a little girl. I was 12, or maybe 13. I'd snuck into someone else's stolen leather jacket. I knew it was stolen, because, well, because I knew who they were. I stole it, from out of the back of a pick-up truck, and then I got in front, and I drove, and I drove, and I drove, all that way to the edge of the pier, and, and I swam to the other side of the sea! On a sunny day like, just to get to the other side, to lie about my age, to fight whatever I thought it could possibly, possibly be. I was wild. I did everything, just to do something.

And all the while that bassline:

We were poor. We were poor. We were poor.

And she, her individuality your image:
She moves against a mechanical army of infinite proportions,
Just so as to open a door, to open that door through which a dream
becomes one of its own.

She does all of this knowing it as a way of waiting,
 for no particular reason.
A way of waiting,
 one which results only in the movement, *faster*, of the material real,
 always toward that same inevitable defeat.

Yet, even without instruction,
Like you, she knew all the rules immediately.
Like you, she went one step too far,
 One beat too quick.

But she leaves behind only an arroyo of matchsticks and spittle, glue and intention; and that vague courageous certainty of children far too often touched.

I click my fingers.
 and she is again that dreamy creature,
 a new neon incarnation, bitter, sweet,
 that doleful agent of the otherwise.

I lick my lips.
In my dreams.

It is only for her,
The piano plays.

All the more.
 And no more.
All the more.
 And no more.
And the bassline kicks in.

> *We were poor.*
> *We were poor.*
> *We were poor.*
> *We were so so poor.*

And though the flowers they have fallen,

Flowers, and fruits, all sorts in blossom,

Figs, berries, and thorns forgotten.

And though the fruit it has long since rotten,

Tending her grave, it remains as pretty as ever.

Each year I sing this better.

Many lines, but one song.

I incant, I recant, I incant and inflame.